ISBN 0 86112 539 8
© Brimax Books Ltd 1989. All rights reserved.
Published by Brimax Books, Newmarket, England 1989.
Printed in Spain.

Big Book of
Nursery Rhymes
and
Fairy Tales

Illustrated by Eric Kincaid

BRIMAX BOOKS • NEWMARKET • ENGLAND

Contents

Nursery Rhymes

Fairy Tales

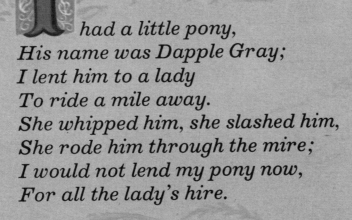

I had a little pony,
His name was Dapple Gray;
I lent him to a lady
To ride a mile away.
She whipped him, she slashed him,
She rode him through the mire;
I would not lend my pony now,
For all the lady's hire.

Oh, the brave old Duke of York,
He had ten thousand men;
He marched them up to the top of the hill,
And he marched them down again.
And when they were up, they were up,
And when they were down, they were down,
And when they were only half-way up,
They were neither up nor down.

The hart he loves the high wood,
The hare she loves the hill;
The knight he loves his bright sword,
The lady loves her will.

Bobby Shafto's gone to sea,
Silver buckles at his knee;
He'll come back and marry me,
Bonny Bobby Shafto!

Bobby Shafto's fat and fair,
Combing down his yellow hair;
He's my love for evermore,
Bonny Bobby Shafto!

A farmer went trotting upon his grey mare,
Bumpety, bumpety, bump!
With his daughter behind him so rosy and fair,
Lumpety, lumpety, lump!

A raven cried, Croak! and they all tumbled down,
Bumpety, bumpety, bump!
The mare broke her knees and the farmer his crown,
Lumpety, lumpety, lump!

The mischievous raven flew laughing away,
Bumpety, bumpety, bump!
And vowed he would serve them the same next day,
Lumpety, lumpety, lump!

Little Robin Redbreast sat upon a tree,
Up went pussy cat, and down went she;
Down came pussy, and away Robin ran;
Says little Robin Redbreast, Catch me if you can.
Little Robin Redbreast jumped upon a wall,
Pussy cat jumped after him, and almost got a fall;
Little Robin chirped and sang, and what did pussy say?
Pussy cat said, Mew, and Robin jumped away.

ary had a little lamb,
It's fleece was white as snow;
And everywhere that Mary went
The lamb was sure to go.

It followed her to school one day,
That was against the rule;
It made the children laugh and play
To see a lamb at school.

And so the teacher turned it out,
But still it lingered near,
And waited patiently about
Till Mary did appear.

Why does the lamb love Mary so?
The eager children cry;
Why, Mary loves the lamb, you know,
The teacher did reply.

Pussy cat Mole jumped over a coal
And in her best petticoat burnt a great hole.
Poor pussy's weeping, she'll have no more milk
Until her best petticoat's mended with silk.

19

The Precious Gift

Once upon a time, there was a King who had three daughters. One day, one of them would be queen. The King could not decide which of them it should be, for they were all beautiful and they were all clever.

"I must make up my mind somehow," he said. "I wonder what I can do?" He thought, and he thought, and at last he made a decision. "I will ask each of my daughters to bring me a gift," he said, "and the one who brings the most precious shall be queen."

On the appointed day he summoned them to the throne room.

The eldest brought a silver bird in a silver cage, which sang when a key was wound.

"A truly beautiful gift," murmured the King.

The second daughter brought a robe of finest silk, trimmed with the softest fur.

"Another truly beautiful gift," murmured the King.

The third daughter brought a plain china bowl which was so small it nestled in the palm of her hand. The King held his breath as he lifted the lid. What precious gift would he find inside it? When the King did see what was in the tiny bowl his face went red, and then it went purple.

"How dare you!" he shouted. He jumped to his feet and threw the little bowl to the floor.

"How dare you insult me by bringing me common salt!"

"But . . . but . . ." The poor little princess tried to say something, but the King shouted and the more he shouted the more angry he became.

"Go!" he shouted. "Go! And never come back. Never! Never! NEVER!"

Of course he was sorry he had said what he did when his temper cooled down, but by then it was too late. The little princess had left the palace.

She wandered sadly until she came to an inn.

"Please let me stay here," she begged. "I have nowhere to go. I will work. I will do anything you ask."

The innkeeper did not know she was a princess or he would have given her his best room and waited on her himself. Instead he sent her down to the kitchen to help the cook.

The cook was a kindly woman. She taught the little princess all she knew about cooking. The princess was quick to learn and before long people were coming to the inn specially to taste her pies and to sample her soups and sauces. The kindly old cook was getting old and gradually the little princess did more and more of the cooking, until soon, she was doing it all.

Everyone who went to the inn talked for days afterwards about the delicious food eaten there, and it was only a matter of time before the King came to hear about the cook who could cook anything, and what was more, cook it perfectly.

"She must come to work in the palace kitchens," he said. "She is the best, and the King always has the best."

And so it was, that the King's own daughter, worked in the palace kitchens and cooked the King's meals, and no one, least of all the King, had any idea who she really was.

The day came when the King's eldest daughter was to be married. Such a hustle and a bustle there was in the palace kitchens. Any banquet is important, but a wedding banquet is the most important of all, especially when a princess is marrying a prince. The little princess, who was now a cook, worked hard and long to get everything prepared.

After the wedding the King and his guests sat down at the tables in the banqueting hall. The King clapped his hands.

"Let the banquet and the merry-making begin," he cried.

The pages and the footmen filed into the hall carrying silver platters piled high with the most delicious food it had ever been the King's privilege to see.

"What a wonderful cook you must have," said a visiting emperor.

The King felt so proud. And then, as was the custom, he lifted his fork and took the first bite of food. Everyone watched, and waited for the sign that they too could begin to eat. To their astonishment the King pulled a face and spat out the food. Princes and princesses, lords and ladies, footmen and pages, stared at the King with open mouths as he tried dish, after dish, scowling harder and harder with each mouthful he tasted. Suddenly he threw down his fork and in a voice like thunder, he shouted,

"FETCH THE COOK!"

He looked so angry everyone trembled, even the visiting emperor, and he didn't frighten easily.

23

"What's wrong? . . . what's wrong? . . ." echoed in whispers round the hall.

The cook came and stood, with her head bowed, in front of the King, who by now was scarlet with rage.

"You have cooked the food without salt!" he roared. "The banquet is ruined! You have shamed me in front of my guests! How dare you forget something so important!"

"But I did not forget," said the cook, who was really a princess. The King was so astonished at a humble cook daring to answer him back he said nothing, and so she was able to continue.

"A long time ago, you banished a daughter because she gave you a gift of common salt . . ."

The King sat down with a bump on his chair. Yes, he did remember that. He had been sorry ever since. But how did the cook know about it? He looked at her closely. She lifted her head so that he could see her face, and smiled. The King jumped to his feet, scattering dishes with a clatter he did not hear.

"Daughter . . ." he cried. "It's you! Can you ever forgive me? You truly gave me a very precious gift and I was too foolish to know it."

Of course the princess forgave her father. And the banquet was not spoilt because she had arranged that only the King's food should be cooked without salt. There was more food already prepared for him in the kitchen.

And so the King and his daughter were reunited and the princess once again took her rightful place in the palace.

Little Tommy Tittlemouse
Lived in a little house;
He caught fishes
In other men's ditches.

Cobbler, cobbler, mend my shoe.
Yes, good master, that I'll do;
Here's my awl and wax and thread,
And now your shoe is quite mended.

Little Polly Flinders
Sat among the cinders,
Warming her pretty little toes;
Her mother came and caught her,
And whipped her little daughter
For spoiling her nice new clothes.

This little pig went to market,
This little pig stayed at home,
This little pig had roast beef,
This little pig had none,
And this little pig cried, Wee-wee-wee-wee-wee,
I can't find my way home.

The cat sat asleep by the side of the fire,
The mistress snored loud as a pig;
Jack took up his fiddle by Jenny's desire,
And struck up a bit of a jig.

Rock-a-bye baby,
Thy cradle is green,
Father's a nobleman,
Mother's a queen;
And Betty's a lady,
And wears a gold ring;
And Johnny's a drummer,
And drums for the king.

When Good King Arthur ruled this land,
He was a goodly king;
He stole three pecks of barley-meal
To make a bag-pudding.

A bag-pudding the king did make,
And stuffed it well with plums;
And in it put great lumps of fat,
As big as my two thumbs.

The king and queen did eat thereof,
And noblemen beside;
And what they could not eat that night,
The queen next morning fried.

There were three jovial Welshmen,
As I have heard men say,
And they would go a-hunting
Upon St. David's Day.

All the day they hunted
And nothing could they find,
But a ship a-sailing,
A-sailing with the wind.

One said it was a ship,
The other he said, Nay;
The third said it was a house,
With the chimney blown away.

And all the night they hunted
And nothing could they find,
But the moon a-gliding,
A-gliding with the wind.

One said it was the moon,
The other he said, Nay;
The third said it was a cheese,
And half of it cut away.

And all the day they hunted
And nothing could they find,
But a hedgehog in a bramble bush,
And that they left behind.

The first said it was a hedgehog,
The second he said, Nay;
The third said it was a pincushion,
And the pins stuck in wrong way.

And all the night they hunted
And nothing could they find,
But a hare in a turnip field,
And that they left behind.

The first said it was a hare,
The second he said, Nay;
The third said it was a calf,
And the cow had run away.

And all the day they hunted
And nothing could they find,
But an owl in a holly tree,
And that they left behind.

One said it was an owl,
The other he said, Nay;
The third said 'twas an old man,
And his beard growing grey.

Jenny Wren fell sick
Upon a merry time,
In came Robin Redbreast
And brought her sops and wine.

Eat well of the sop, Jenny,
Drink well of the wine.
Thank you, Robin, kindly,
You shall be mine.

Jenny Wren got well,
And stood upon her feet;
And told Robin plainly,
She loved him not a bit.

Robin he got angry,
And hopped upon a twig,
Saying, Out upon you, fie upon you!
Bold faced jig!

33

I had a little hobby horse, it was well shod,
It carried me to London, niddety nod,
And when we got to London we heard a great shout,
Down fell my hobby horse and I cried out:
Up again, hobby horse, if thou be a beast,
When we get to our town we will have a feast,
And if there is but little, why thou shalt have some,
And dance to the bag-pipes and beating of the drum.

See-saw, Margery Daw,
Jacky shall have a new master;
Jacky shall have but a penny a day,
Because he can't work any faster.

Diddle, diddle, dumpling, my son John,
Went to bed with his trousers on;
One shoe off, and one shoe on,
Diddle, diddle, dumpling, my son John.

Handy Spandy, Jack-a-Dandy,
Loves plum cake and sugar candy;
He bought some at a grocer's shop,
And out he came, hop, hop, hop, hop.

A wise old owl lived in an oak;
The more he saw the less he spoke;
The less he spoke the more he heard.
Why can't we all be like that wise old bird?

The cock's on the wood pile a-blowing his horn,
The bull's in the barn a-threshing of corn,
The maids in the meadows are making the hay,
The ducks in the river are swimming away.

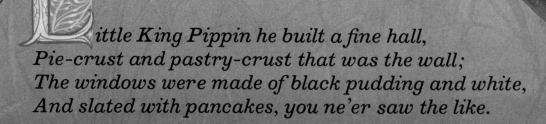

Little King Pippin he built a fine hall,
Pie-crust and pastry-crust that was the wall;
The windows were made of black pudding and white,
And slated with pancakes, you ne'er saw the like.

The Emperor's New Clothes

Once there was an Emperor who was always changing his clothes. He had a different outfit for every hour of the day. Whenever his ministers wanted him for something special, they always went to the royal clothes closet first. He was more likely to be there deciding what to change into next, than passing laws in his Council Chamber, or balancing the budget in his Counting House.

One day, two men arrived in town. They knew how fond the Emperor was of new clothes and they had hatched a plan. A crafty plan. They spread the news that they could weave the most beautiful cloth anyone had ever seen, and furthermore it was magic, and invisible to anyone who was stupid, or unworthy of the position he held.

"I must have an outfit made from that marvellous new cloth everyone is talking about," said the Emperor, and he sent for the weavers. They agreed to weave some of the cloth for him and went away from the palace carrying silk and golden thread, as well as a large sum of money.

They hid the silk and golden thread in their packs and then set up their loom. There was the steady clack, clack, and the whirr of a busy loom for days. The Emperor was very anxious to see how the new cloth was coming along, but he was just a tiny bit afraid.

'What would I do if I could not see the cloth?' he thought. And though he didn't think for a moment that he wasn't fit to be emperor, he sent his faithful old Prime Minister to look at the cloth in his place.

The weavers led the Prime Minister to their loom. He could not see a single thread.

'Oh dear,' he thought, 'If the Emperor finds out I can't see the cloth I will lose my job. I must pretend I CAN see it.'

"It's the most beautiful piece of cloth in the world," he told the Emperor on his return to the palace.

The Emperor decided perhaps he would go and see it for himself after all. He gathered his favourite councillors around him and went to the weavers.

"Show us our beautiful new cloth," he said.

"Can you not see it? It's there, on the loom," said the weavers.

"So it is . . . so it is . . ." said the Emperor, his voice full of admiration and his heart full of shame, because HE could not see the cloth either. But then neither could anyone else, though everyone THOUGHT everyone else could see it. There were so many exclamations of delight at the beauty of the new cloth, it really was quite astonishing, in the circumstances.

"Make me a suit of clothes from the cloth and I will wear it in procession tomorrow," said the Emperor, outwardly smiling, and inwardly trembling.

The two weavers said they were tailors too, and that they would make the suit themselves. At eight o'clock next morning it was ready. Or so they told the Emperor.

The Emperor bathed. He powdered his hair. He put on his shoes and stockings. And then he let the weavers dress him in the new suit of clothes.

"It's a perfect fit," they said.

"It's a perfect fit," said ALL the councillors.

"It's a perfect fit," said the Emperor, although he could see nothing but his own pink skin.

When the Emperor was ready, or thought he was, the procession through the streets of the town began. Everyone knew about the wonderful cloth. Everyone knew that only those worthy enough could see it, and that to everyone else it was invisible.

"Look at the Emperor's new suit . . . isn't it beautiful . . ?" sighed the people in the crowd as he walked proudly by.

"How well it fits . . ."

"Ahhh . . . truly a suit fit for an emperor . . ."

And then a little voice rang out above the others. It belonged to a boy who never listened to gossip and he hadn't heard the stories about the wonderful cloth, besides his father had taught him always to be truthful.

"The Emperor has no clothes on!" he shouted.

Someone began to laugh. "The boy's right! The Emperor has no clothes on!"

The cry was caught up by the people in the crowd.

"The Emperor has no clothes on . . ."

The poor Emperor was shivering with cold so he knew the crowd must be right, but he walked proudly through the streets and back to the palace with his head held high and his skin blushing a bright and glowing crimson.

He sent guards to fetch the weavers so that they could be punished for daring to trick an emperor, but they had vanished and were never seen again. And from that day onwards, I'm glad to say, the Emperor paid a little less attention to what he wore, and more attention to the affairs of state.

Little Tommy Tucker,
Sings for his supper:
What shall we give him?
White bread and butter.
How shall he cut it
Without a knife?
How will he be married
Without a wife?

One, two, three, four, five,
Once I caught a fish alive,
Six, seven, eight, nine, ten,
Then I let it go again.

Why did you let it go?
Because it bit my finger so.
Which finger did it bite?
This little finger on the right.

I love little pussy,
Her coat is so warm,
And if I don't hurt her
She'll do me no harm.
So I'll not pull her tail,
Nor drive her away,
But pussy and I
Very gently will play.

Humpty Dumpty sat on a wall,
Humpty Dumpty had a great fall.
All the king's horses,
And all the king's men,
Couldn't put Humpty together again.

Hark, hark,
The dogs do bark,
The beggars are coming to town;
Some in rags,
And some in jags,
And one in a velvet gown.

46

The Owl and the Pussy-cat went to sea
In a beautiful pea-green boat,
They took some honey, and plenty of money,
Wrapped up in a five-pound note.
The Owl looked up to the stars above,
And sang to a small guitar,
'O lovely Pussy! Pussy, my love,
What a beautiful Pussy you are,
    You are,
    You are!
What a beautiful Pussy you are!'

Pussy said to the Owl, 'You elegant fowl!
How charmingly sweet you sing!
O let us be married! too long we have tarried:
But what shall we do for a ring?'
They sailed away, for a year and a day,
To the land where the Bong-tree grows,
And there in a wood a Piggy-wig stood
With a ring at the end of his nose,
  His nose,
  His nose,
With a ring at the end of his nose.

'Dear Pig, are you willing to sell for one shilling
Your ring?' Said the Piggy, 'I will'.
So they took it away, and were married next day
By the Turkey who lives on the hill.
They dined on mince, and slices of quince,
Which they ate with a runcible spoon;
And hand in hand, on the edge of the sand,
They danced by the light of the moon,
  The moon,
  The moon,
They danced by the light of the moon.

There was an old woman who lived in a shoe,
She had so many children she didn't know what to do;
She gave them some broth without any bread;
She whipped them all soundly and put them to bed.

Ladybird, ladybird,
Fly away home,
Your house is on fire
And your children all gone;
All except one
And that's little Ann
And she has crept under
The warming pan.

ing the bells, ring!
Hip, hurrah for the King!
The dunce fell into the pool, oh!
The dunce was going to school, oh!
The groom and the cook
Fished him out with a hook,
And he piped his eye like a fool, oh!

Punch and Judy
Fought for a pie;
Punch gave Judy
A knock in the eye.
Says Punch to Judy
Will you have any more?
Says Judy to Punch,
My eye is sore.

 ere am I,
Little Jumping Joan;
When nobody's with me
I'm all alone.

 ld Mother Shuttle
Lived in a coal-scuttle
Along with her dog and her cat;
What they ate I can't tell,
But 'tis known very well
That not one of the party was fat.

Old Mother Shuttle
Scoured out her coal-scuttle,
And washed both her dog and her cat;
The cat scratched her nose,
So they came to hard blows,
And who was the gainer by that?

Who killed Cock Robin?
I, said the Sparrow,
With my bow and arrow,
I killed Cock Robin.

Who saw him die?
I, said the Fly,
With my little eye,
I saw him die.

Who caught his blood?
I, said the Fish,
With my little dish,
I caught his blood.

Who'll make the shroud?
I, said the Beetle,
With my thread and needle,
I'll make the shroud.

Who'll dig his grave?
I, said the Owl,
With my pick and shovel,
I'll dig his grave.

Who'll be the parson?
I, said the Rook,
With my little book,
I'll be the parson.

Who'll be the clerk?
I, said the Lark,
If it's not in the dark,
I'll be the clerk.

Who'll carry the link?
I, said the Linnet,
I'll fetch it in a minute,
I'll carry the link.

Who'll be chief mourner?
I, said the Dove,
I mourn for my love,
I'll be chief mourner.

Who'll carry the coffin?
I, said the Kite,
If it's not through the night,
I'll carry the coffin.

Who'll bear the pall?
We, said the Wren,
Both the cock and the hen,
We'll bear the pall.

Who'll sing a psalm?
I, said the Thrush,
As she sat on a bush,
I'll sing a psalm.

Who'll toll the bell?
I, said the Bull,
Because I can pull,
I'll toll the bell.

All the birds of the air
Fell a-sighing and a-sobbing,
When they heard the bell toll
For poor Cock Robin.

Mary, Mary, quite contrary,
How does your garden grow?
With silver bells and cockle shells,
And pretty maids all in a row.

Hickory, dickory, dock,
The mouse ran up the clock.
The clock struck one,
The mouse ran down,
Hickory, dickory, dock.

57

Twelve Dancing Princesses

Once upon a time, there was a King who had twelve beautiful daughters, and an unusual problem. Every night, when the twelve princesses were sent to bed their shoes were perfectly sound. Every morning when they came down to breakfast their shoes were full of holes. Every day the King had to buy twelve pairs of new shoes. That was expensive, though the expense did not worry the King. What did worry him was not knowing WHY the shoes were full of holes.

He tried locking the bedroom door on the outside when all the princesses were safely inside, and sleeping with the key under his pillow. It made no difference. The princesses' shoes were still full of holes in the morning.

The King was so puzzled, and so vexed, because he couldn't find out WHY it was happening that he issued a proclamation.

It said, WHOMSOEVER SHALL DISCOVER WHY THE PRINCESSES' SHOES ARE FULL OF HOLES EVERY MORNING SHALL HAVE ONE OF THE PRINCESSES FOR HIS WIFE AND SHALL INHERIT MY KINGDOM WHEN I DIE.

Princes came from far and wide to try to find an answer to the mystery. Not one of them succeeded. The puzzled King was beginning to despair of ever finding an answer when a poor soldier came to the palace. The proclamation had said nothing about being a prince if you wanted to solve the mystery, so he had decided to make an attempt at it himself.

The King received the soldier as kindly, and as grandly, as any of the Princes, and that night he was taken to a room adjoining the princesses' bedroom so that he could keep watch.

Now it so happened, that the soldier had been kind to a wise old woman on his way to the palace, and she had given him a cloak, and some advice. "When the princesses offer you wine," she had said, "pretend to drink it and then pretend to fall asleep. Wear the cloak when you want to be invisible."

That night, when the princesses were ready for bed, the eldest said to the soldier,

"You must be thirsty. Take this cup of wine and drink."

The soldier remembered the wise woman's words and pretended to drink. And then, he pretended to get drowsy. Presently he closed his eyes as though he was asleep.

As soon as they heard him snore the princesses jumped from their beds and put on their shoes and their prettiest dresses.

"Are you all ready?" asked the eldest.

"We are ready," replied her sisters.

The eldest princess pressed a carved leaf on the end of her bed. The bed moved slowly to one side and revealed a hidden staircase leading down into the earth. The princesses picked up their skirts and hurried down the steps, the eldest leading the way, and the youngest following last of all.

The soldier, who of course was awake and had seen everything, put the cloak the old woman had given him round his shoulders. It covered him from head to toe and made him completely invisible.

He ran after the princesses and caught up with them at the bottom of the steps. He was in such a hurry not to be left behind that he accidentally stepped on the hem of the youngest princess's dress, and tore it.

"Oh . . ." she gasped. "Someone has stepped on my dress."

"Don't be silly," said her sisters. "You caught it on a nail . . . come hurry . . . we must not be late."

At the bottom of the steps there was a wood in which all the trees had silver leaves. The soldier broke off one, and put it in his pocket.

"What was that?" cried the youngest princess in alarm, as she heard the snap of the breaking twig.

"It was nothing . . ." said her sisters.

Next, they passed through an avenue in which all the trees had golden leaves. Again the princess heard the snap of a breaking twig, but again her sisters told her it was her own imagination playing tricks on her.

The running princesses came to the shores of a wide blue lake. At the edge of the lake were twelve boats, with twelve handsome princes sitting, waiting, at the oars. The soldier sat in the boat which was to carry the youngest princess.

"I wonder what makes the boat so heavy today," said the prince, as he pulled, harder than usual, at the oars.

On the far side of the lake there was a magnificent palace from which the sounds of music and merry-making came . . . and it was there that the mystery of the worn out shoes was solved. The twelve princesses danced the entire night with the twelve handsome princes.

Just before dawn, and when all their shoes were in shreds, the princes rowed the princesses back across the lake, and the princesses ran home.

As soon as they reached their bedroom they hurried to look at the soldier. He had run home ahead of them and they found him on his bed, still sleeping, or so they thought.

"We are safe . . ." said the eldest princess.

The soldier followed the princesses to the secret palace the next night, and the following night too. On the third night he took the jewelled cup from which the youngest princess drank and slipped it into a pocket in the invisible cloak.

On the morning after the third night, the King sent for the soldier, and said,

"Your time is up. Either tell me why my daughters' shoes are worn through every morning, or be banished forever . . ."

"Your daughters' shoes are worn because they dance every night in an underground palace," said the soldier, and he told the King all that he had seen.

The princesses gasped and turned pale as the soldier took the silver leaf, the golden leaf, and the jewelled cup from his pocket and handed them to the King. They knew now they could not deny that what the soldier said was true.

"We must confess," said the eldest princess.

The King was so relieved to have the mystery of the worn shoes explained, he couldn't stay cross with his daughters for long.

"Now I shall be able to sleep at night," he said.

The King kept the promise he had made in the proclamation, and the soldier married the princess of his choice. And many years later, when the old King died, he became King in his place.

How many days has my baby to play?
Saturday, Sunday, Monday,
Tuesday, Wednesday, Thursday, Friday,
Saturday, Sunday, Monday.
Hop away, skip away,
My baby wants to play,
My baby wants to play every day.

The dove says, Coo, coo, what shall I do?
I can scarce maintain two.
Pooh, pooh, says the wren, I have ten,
And keep them all like gentlemen.

Tommy Trot a man of law,
Sold his bed and lay upon straw;
Sold the straw and slept on grass,
To buy his wife a looking glass.

I do not like thee, Doctor Fell,
The reason why I cannot tell;
But this I know, and know full well,
I do not like thee, Doctor Fell.

The fiddler and his wife,
The piper and his mother,
Ate three half-cakes, three whole cakes,
And three quarters of another.

ld Mother Hubbard
Went to the cupboard,
To fetch her poor dog a bone;
But when she came there
The cupboard was bare
And so the poor dog had none.

She went to the baker's
To buy him some bread;
But when she came back
The poor dog was dead.

She went to the undertaker's
To buy him a coffin;
But when she came back
The poor dog was laughing.

She took a clean dish
To get him some tripe;
But when she came back
He was smoking a pipe.

She went to the alehouse
To get him some beer;
But when she came back
The dog sat in a chair.

She went to the tavern
For white wine and red;
But when she came back
The dog stood on his head.

She went to the fruiterer's
To buy him some fruit;
But when she came back
He was playing the flute.

She went to the tailor's
To buy him a coat;
But when she came back
He was riding a goat.

She went to the hatter's
To buy him a hat;
But when she came back
He was feeding the cat.

She went to the barber's
To buy him a wig;
But when she came back
He was dancing a jig.

She went to the cobbler's
To buy him some shoes;
But when she came back
He was reading the news.

She went to the seamstress
To buy him some linen;
But when she came back
The dog was a-spinning.

She went to the hosier's
To buy him some hose;
But when she came back
He was dressed in his clothes.

The dame made a curtsy,
The dog made a bow;
The dame said, Your servant,
The dog said, Bow-wow.

Bessy Bell and Mary Gray,
They were two bonny lasses;
They built their house upon the lea,
And covered it with rushes.

Bessy kept the garden gate,
And Mary kept the pantry;
Bessy always had to wait,
While Mary lived in plenty.

Yankee Doodle came to town,
Riding on a pony;
He stuck a feather in his cap
And called it macaroni.

There was a little girl, and she had a little curl
Right in the middle of her forehead;
When she was good, she was very, very good,
But when she was bad, she was horrid.

Thumbling

There are many stories about Thumbling, the boy who was no bigger than a thumb. All adventures have to begin somewhere, and this story tells how one of Thumbling's began.

Thumbling's father was going into the forest to cut wood.

"I do wish someone could bring the cart to me when I have finished," he sighed, "then I wouldn't have to come all the way home to fetch it."

"I'll bring it to you," said Thumbling.

"How can you?" laughed Thumbling's father. "You are far too small to lead the horse."

"That may be so," said Thumbling, "but if Mother harnesses the horse for me I will sit in his ear, and tell him where to go."

It seemed a good idea, so Thumbling's father went off with his axe over his shoulder. "Make sure you're not late," he said.

"I won't be," said Thumbling.

When it was time, Thumbling's mother harnessed the horse, Thumbling climbed into the horse's ear, and off they went.

"Gee up!" cried Thumbling, who for such a small boy had an astonishingly loud voice. "Gee up!" The horse wasn't too keen on being shouted at from inside his own ear and set off at a brisk trot. "To the right!" shouted Thumbling, when he wanted the horse to go to the right. "To the left!" shouted Thumbling when he wanted him to go to the left. "Straight on!" he shouted when he wanted him to go neither to the left, nor to the right. They were almost at the place where they were to meet Thumbling's father, when they passed two men.

"That's very strange," said one of the men. "I can hear the driver of that horse and cart, but I can't see him."

"Let's follow it, and see where it goes," said his companion.

"Whoa there . . ." shouted Thumbling when they reached the clearing. "Are we in good time?"

"I've just finished," said Thumbling's father, as he lifted Thumbling from the horse's ear.

The two men nearly fell over one another in their excitement.

"If we had a little man like that we could make our fortunes," they cried. "We could show him at the fairgrounds. People would come from miles around to see him. We must buy him."

"No!" said Thumbling's father when they spoke to him. "My son is not for sale."

Now it so happened that Thumbling felt in the right mood to start a new adventure, so he climbed onto his father's shoulder and whispered,

"Let me go Father. You and Mother could use the money, and I will come back. You can be sure of that."

So, Thumbling's father, who was used to his son's ways, said the two men could take him in exchange for a bag of gold, and if they first helped him load the logs onto the cart.

"Where will you sit?" asked one of the men, when Thumbling had waved goodbye to his father.

"On the brim of your hat," said Thumbling.

"Is he still there?" asked the man who was wearing the hat, every few minutes. Because he was wearing the hat he couldn't see what was happening on the brim.

"We mustn't lose him."

Sometimes, when they checked Thumbling was at the front of the hat. Sometimes he was at the back. Sometimes he was looking where they were going. Sometimes he was looking where they had been. Sometimes he was lying on his back, looking up at the endless blue sky.

The two men walked a long way. Just as it was beginning to get dark, they sat down on a grassy bank to rest.

"Take your hat off," said Thumbling.

"Why should I do that?" asked the man wearing the hat.

"Because it's bad manners to keep your hat on ALL the time," said Thumbling. "And anyway, if you don't take your hat off sometimes your head will get too hot and your hair will fall out."

"You could be right," said the man, and took off his hat and laid it on the grass.

Quick as a grasshopper, Thumbling jumped off the brim, and ran through the grass until he came to a mousehole. Down he went.

The two men were furious.

"Come out!" they shouted. "We have been tricked!" they shouted even louder. It didn't matter how much they shouted, or how hard they poked their sticks down the mousehole, Thumbling would NOT come out. Eventually it became too dark to see where the hole was any more and they had to go home without him.

Now Thumbling was free to go where he wanted and do what he liked. He slept in the mousehole that night and next day he went to look for adventure. It was a long time before he got home again, but he did get there in the end. He always did at the end of ALL his adventures.

Cackle, cackle, Mother Goose,
Have you any feathers loose?
Truly have I, pretty fellow,
Half enough to fill a pillow.
Here are quills, take one or two,
And down to make a bed for you.

As I was going along,
long, long,
A-singing a comical song,
song, song,
The lane that I went was so
long, long, long,
And the song that I sung
was as long, long, long,
And so I went singing along.

saw a ship a-sailing,
A-sailing on the sea,
And oh but it was laden
With pretty things for thee.

There were comfits in the cabin,
And apples in the hold;
The sails were made of silk,
And the masts were all of gold.

The four-and-twenty sailors,
That stood between the decks,
Were four-and-twenty white mice
With chains about their necks.

The captain was a duck
With a packet on his back,
And when the ship began to move
The captain said Quack! Quack!

This is the house that Jack built.

This is the malt
That lay in the house that Jack built.

This is the rat,
That ate the malt
That lay in the house that Jack built.

This is the cat,
That killed the rat,
That ate the malt
That lay in the house that Jack built.

This is the dog,
That worried the cat,
That killed the rat,
That ate the malt
That lay in the house that Jack built.

This is the cow with the crumpled horn,
That tossed the dog,
That worried the cat,
That killed the rat,
That ate the malt
That lay in the house that Jack built.

This is the maiden all forlorn,
That milked the cow with the crumpled horn,
That tossed the dog,
That worried the cat,
That killed the rat,
That ate the malt
That lay in the house that Jack built.

This is the man all tattered and torn,
That kissed the maiden all forlorn,
That milked the cow with the crumpled horn,
That tossed the dog,
That worried the cat,
That killed the rat,
That ate the malt
That lay in the house that Jack built.

This is the priest all shaven and shorn,
That married the man all tattered and torn,
That kissed the maiden all forlorn,
That milked the cow with the crumpled horn,
That tossed the dog,
That worried the cat,
That killed the rat,
That ate the malt
That lay in the house that Jack built.

This is the cock that crowed in the morn,
That waked the priest all shaven and shorn,
That married the man all tattered and torn,
That kissed the maiden all forlorn,
That milked the cow with the crumpled horn,
That tossed the dog,
That worried the cat,
That killed the rat,
That ate the malt
That lay in the house that Jack built.

This is the farmer sowing his corn,
That kept the cock that crowed in the morn,
That waked the priest all shaven and shorn,
That married the man all tattered and torn,
That kissed the maiden all forlorn,
That milked the cow with the crumpled horn,
That tossed the dog,
That worried the cat,
That killed the rat,
That ate the malt
That lay in the house that Jack built.

Bye, baby bunting,
Daddy's gone a-hunting,
Gone to get a rabbit skin
To wrap the baby bunting in.

Tom, he was a piper's son,
He learnt to play when he was young,
And all the tune that he could play
Was, 'Over the hills and far away';
Over the hills and a great way off,
The wind shall blow my top-knot off.

Tom with his pipe made such a noise,
That he pleased both the girls and boys,
And they all stopped to hear him play,
'Over the hills and far away'.

Tom with his pipe did play with such skill
That those who heard him could never keep still;
As soon as he played they began for to dance,
Even pigs on their hind legs would after him prance.

Peter White will ne'er go right;
Would you know the reason why?
He follows his nose wherever he goes,
And that stands all awry.

Doctor Foster went to Gloucester
In a shower of rain;
He stepped in a puddle,
Right up to his middle,
And never went there again.

*T*hree little kittens they lost their mittens,
And they began to cry,
Oh, mother dear, we sadly fear
That we have lost our mittens.
What! LOST YOUR MITTENS, YOU NAUGHTY KITTENS!
Then you shall have no pie.
Mee-ow, mee-ow, mee-ow.
No, you shall have no pie.

The three little kittens they found their mittens,
And they began to cry,
Oh, mother dear, see here, see here,
For we have found our mittens.
Put on your mittens, you silly kittens,
And you shall have some pie.
Purr-r, purr-r, purr-r,
Oh, let us have some pie.

The three little kittens put on their mittens,
And soon ate up the pie;
Oh, mother dear, we greatly fear
That we have soiled our mittens.
What! soiled your mittens, you naughty kittens!
Then they began to sigh.
Mee-ow, mee-ow, mee-ow.
Then they began to sigh.

The three little kittens they washed their mittens,
And hung them out to dry;
Oh! mother dear, do you not hear
That we have washed our mittens?
What! washed your mittens, then you're good kittens,
But I smell a rat close by.
Mee-ow, mee-ow, mee-ow.
We smell a rat close by.

eter Piper picked a peck of pickled pepper;
A peck of pickled pepper Peter Piper picked;
If Peter Piper picked a peck of pickled pepper,
Where's the peck of pickled pepper Peter Piper picked?

Rapunzel

One day, a Prince was riding in the forest when he heard a girl singing. He got down from his horse and led him quietly along a mossy footpath until he came to a clearing. In the clearing was a tower, as round and as straight as a giant pine tree. At the very top of the tower, which was so tall it looked as though its roof was touching the sky, there was a tiny window. It was from the tiny window that the sound of the voice was coming.

"It will be a long climb up the stairs to the top," said the Prince shading his eyes and looking upwards, "but I must find out who is singing so sweetly."

He looped the horse's bridle over a branch and went to look for a way in. He walked round the tower a hundred times. He could find no door . . . no window . . . no hidden entrance. It was impossible to climb up the outside for the sides were so smooth there was neither crack nor ledge where he could put his feet. In the end the disappointed Prince had to give up his quest and ride home with the sound of the voice drifting in the wind behind him.

The Prince could not forget the voice. He dreamed about it in daydreams and dreamed about it in his sleep. He rode into the forest every day, just to hear it.

One day, when he was sitting in the branches of the tree closest to the tower, an old witch came out of the forest. The Prince kept very quiet and watched to see what she would do.

She went to the foot of the tower, and called,

"Rapunzel, Rapunzel, let down your hair."

Immediately, a long braid of golden hair tumbled from the window at the top of the tower. It was so long, its tip touched the ground. The old witch caught hold of it as though it was a rope and someone, in the room at the top of the tower, pulled her upwards until she disappeared.

The Prince was so excited he almost fell out of the tree. He waited until the old witch had come down again and hobbled away into the forest, then he went to the foot of the tower himself.

"Rapunzel, Rapunzel," he called. "Let down your hair."

Again the golden hair came tumbling from the tower, but this time it was a handsome prince who used it as a rope and not an ugly old witch. In the tiny room at the top of the tower was the most beautiful girl he had ever seen.

"Who . . . who . . . are you?" she gasped as he climbed over the windowsill and into the room. "I thought you were the witch."

"Do not be afraid," said the Prince, "I will not hurt you."

He told her his name and how he had heard her singing when he was riding in the forest.

"I sing because I am lonely," said Rapunzel. "I have been locked alone in this tower since I was twelve years old. My only visitor is the witch who brought me here."

"I will help you escape," said the Prince.

"How can you?" sighed Rapunzel. "I cannot climb down my own hair and there is no other way in, or out of, the tower."

"I will bring you a silken ladder," promised the Prince.

That evening the old witch visited Rapunzel again.

"You are much heavier than the Prince," said Rapunzel, without thinking of the consequences of her words. "Why is that?"

The witch was so angry she almost exploded. She had locked Rapunzel in the tower to keep her away from handsome princes. She wanted Rapunzel to love no one in the world but herself. She snatched a pair of scissors from the table, and before Rapunzel could stop her she had cut off her long braids of golden hair.

"Now your Prince will never get into the tower," screamed the witch. And then, because she really was very angry indeed, she banished Rapunzel to a far-away place. Even if the Prince did find a way into the tower, Rapunzel would not be there.

The Prince had no way of knowing what had happened of course, and the next day, when he called to Rapunzel to let down her hair, he thought it was she who threw the long golden braids over the windowsill. But it was not. It was the witch. It was the witch who pulled the Prince upwards . . . and upwards . . . and upwards.

"You will never see Rapunzel again!" she screamed, as the Prince looked over the windowsill and straight into her ugly face. And with that terrible cry, she let go the braids, so that they, and the Prince, fell to the ground.

The Prince was bumped and bruised, and when at last he stirred, and opened his eyes, he could not see. He was blind.

The Prince thought Rapunzel was locked in the tower with the witch and though he tried, he could find no way of helping her. He wandered about the countryside, blind, lonely and unhappy.

And then one day, just by chance, he came to the place where Rapunzel was living. He heard her singing and, though her voice was as sad as a flower without petals, he recognized it at once.

"Rapunzel," he called softly. "Is that you?"

Rapunzel was overjoyed, but when she saw the Prince's poor blind eyes, she wept hot, splashing tears. Some of her tears fell onto the Prince's face. Suddenly he could see. Her tears had broken the witch's terrible spell.

Rapunzel and the Prince were married and lived happily ever after. And as for the old witch, she was never heard of, or seen again. Perhaps she is still locked in the tower. Once she had let go of the braids she had no way of getting out of the tower herself, had she?

There was an old woman
Lived under a hill,
And if she's not gone
She lives there still.

Little Bo-peep has lost her sheep,
And can't tell where to find them;
Leave them alone, and they'll come home,
And bring their tails behind them.

Little Bo-peep fell fast asleep,
And dreamt she heard them bleating;
But when she awoke, she found it a joke,
For they were still all fleeting.

Then up she took her little crook,
Determined for to find them;
She found them indeed, but it made her heart bleed,
For they'd left their tails behind them.

It happened one day, as Bo-peep did stray
Into a meadow hard by,
There she espied their tails side by side,
All hung on a tree to dry.

She heaved a sigh, and wiped her eye,
And over the hillocks went rambling,
And tried what she could, as a shepherdess should,
To tack again each to its lambkin.

When I was a little boy I lived by myself,
And all the bread and cheese I got I laid upon a shelf;
The rats and the mice they made such a strife,
I had to go to London town and buy me a wife.

The streets were so broad and the lanes were so narrow,
I was forced to bring my wife home in a wheelbarrow.
The wheelbarrow broke and my wife had a fall,
Farewell wheelbarrow, little wife and all.

Hickety, pickety, my black hen,
She lays eggs for gentlemen;
Gentlemen come every day
To see what my black hen doth lay.
Sometimes nine and sometimes ten,
Hickety, pickety, my black hen.

Mr. East gave a feast;
Mr. North laid the cloth;
Mr. West did his best;
Mr. South burnt his mouth
With eating a cold potato.

The Pedlar of Swaffham

Once, long ago, when London Bridge was lined with shops, a pedlar living in the country, far away from London, had a strange dream. He dreamed that if he went to London Bridge he would hear some good news. The first time he had the dream he didn't take much notice of it. The second time he had the dream he began to wonder, and the third time he had the dream, he decided to make the trip to London Town.

He was too poor to hire a horse and it was a very long walk. His shoes had almost worn out by the time he got there.

He walked up and down the bridge for three days waiting to hear what the good news might be. On the third day, one of the shopkeepers who kept a shop on the bridge could bear it no longer. He left his wife to serve the customers and went to speak to the pedlar.

"I've watched you walk up and down for three whole days," he said. "Have you something to sell?"

"No," said the pedlar.

"Then are you begging?" asked the shopkeeper, looking at his worn shoes and dusty coat.

"Certainly not," said the pedlar.

"Then what ARE you doing?" asked the shopkeeper.

The pedlar told him about his dream.

The shopkeeper hooted with merry laughter. "Do you mean to say you have come all this way because of a dream? I dream myself. Why only last night I dreamed that in an orchard behind a pedlar's house in Swaffham, which is a place I've never even heard of, there is an oak tree, and under the oak tree there is a buried treasure . . . now do you think I would be so foolish as to leave my shop and go all the way to a place I've never heard of, just because I had a dream . . . hey . . . where are you going?"

"Home," called the pedlar over his shoulder.

"What a strange fellow," said the shopkeeper, and went back to his shop shaking his head over the peculiarity of people. How was he to know that the pedlar lived in a place called Swaffham and that there was an orchard behind HIS house.

Even walking quickly it took several days for the pedlar to get home, but as soon as he was there he went into the orchard and started to dig. Sure enough, he found a chest of buried treasure and a dream came true.

And so the pedlar was rich until the end of his days and all because of a dream. Or rather two dreams. If he had not taken heed of his own dream he would not have heard the shopkeeper's dream, and no doubt the treasure which made him rich would be buried still.

Once I saw a little bird
Come hop, hop, hop,
And I cried, Little bird,
Will you stop, stop, stop?

I was going to the window
To say, How do you do?
But he shook his little tail
And away he flew.

One, two,
Buckle my shoe;
Three, four,
Knock at the door;
Five, six,
Pick up sticks;
Seven, eight,
Lay them straight;
Nine, ten,
A big fat hen;
Eleven, twelve,
Dig and delve;
Thirteen, fourteen,
Maids a-courting;
Fifteen, sixteen,
Maids in the kitchen;
Seventeen, eighteen,
Maids in waiting;
Nineteen, twenty,
My plate's empty.

As I was going up the hill,
I met with Jack the piper;
And all the tune that he could play
Was, 'Tie up your petticoats tighter'.

I tied them once, I tied them twice,
I tied them three times over;
And all the song that he could sing
Was, 'Carry me safe to Dover'.

Three wise men of Gotham,
They went to sea in a bowl,
And if the bowl had been stronger
My song had been longer.

here was a man and he had nought,
And robbers came to rob him;
He crept up to the chimney top,
And then they thought they had him.

But he got down on the other side,
And then they could not find him;
He ran fourteen miles in fifteen days,
And never looked behind him.

112

One, two, three, four,
Mary at the cottage door,
Five, six, seven, eight,
Eating cherries off a plate.

The Three Spinners

Once there was a girl who could not spin thread. She could do other things, but she could not, or would not, spin. It made her mother very angry to see her sitting idle at the spinning wheel.

"You lazy, lazy girl," she would shout, and then she would hit the girl across the shoulders.

One day, when she was shouting, and the girl was sitting crying at the spinning wheel, the Queen happened to pass by in her coach. She heard the girl crying and called to her coachman to stop the horses.

"Why are you beating your daughter?" she asked. "Why are you shouting at her? Why is she crying? What has she done?"

A Queen's questions should always be answered truthfully, but the old woman was too ashamed to say she thought her daughter was lazy, so she said instead,

"My daughter loves to spin. I am only a poor old woman and I cannot afford to buy the flax. She cries because she wants to spin . . . I do not know what to do."

"Your troubles are over," said the Queen, who as it happened, loved to hear the whirr of the spinning wheel and to see freshly spun thread. "I have plenty of flax at the palace. I will take your daughter home with me and she can spin as much as she likes."

The Queen took the girl to the palace and showed her three rooms which were full from floor to ceiling with unspun flax.

"Spin all THAT flax into thread, my dear, and you shall marry my son," said the Queen.

The poor girl did not know what to do. Of course she wanted to marry the prince, but how could she? She didn't know HOW to spin. For three whole days she sat and wept. On the third day the Queen came to see her.

"Why are you weeping child? Why haven't you started to spin?" asked the Queen.

The poor girl sobbed even harder.

"I brought you to the palace to spin flax," said the Queen sternly. "If there is no thread for me to see tomorrow you will be punished."

When the Queen had swept majestically from the room, the poor, sad girl stood at the window overlooking the street and cried as though her heart would break. Presently, through her tears, she saw three strange women walking along the pavement. One of them had a very broad, flat foot. One had a lip that hung down over her chin, and the third had an enormous thumb.

One of the women called up to the window and asked the girl why she was weeping.

"I do so want to marry the prince," she sobbed, "But first I must spin all this flax, and I do not know how to spin."

"If you will call us aunt and be unashamed of our strange appearance, and if you will invite us to sit with you at your wedding, we will help you," said the three women.

"I shall be glad to call you aunt," said the girl.

The three strange women were as good as their word. They slipped unnoticed into the palace and set to work. The one with the broad, flat foot worked the spinning wheel. The one with the lip which hung over her chin wetted the flax. And the one with the enormous thumb twisted the thread. Together they spun the finest thread the Queen had ever seen. She was impressed, though she thought the girl herself had done the spinning for the three strange women hid whenever they heard the Queen coming.

At last all the flax had been spun and it was time for the wedding. When the arrangements were being made, the girl said to the Queen,

"I have three aunts who have been very kind to me. May I invite them to the wedding and may they sit with me at the table?"

"Of course," said the Queen.

An invitation was sent, and on the day of the wedding the three strange women arrived and were welcomed kindly by the girl and the Prince.

"Tell me Aunt," said the Prince, who couldn't help noticing such things. "Why have you such a broad flat foot?"

"Because I tread a spinning wheel," said the first aunt.

"And how is it that you have such a long lip?" he asked the second aunt.

"Because I wet the spinning thread."

"And why have you such a large thumb?" asked the Prince of the third aunt.

"Because I twist the spinning thread," she answered.

The Prince looked at the three strange women, one with a broad flat foot, one with a lip that hung down over her chin and one with an enormous thumb, and then he looked at his beautiful bride.

"If that is what spinning thread does to a woman," he said, "I forbid you ever to touch a spinning wheel."

And so the girl married her prince, and the three spinners moved into the palace to take care of all the spinning. They loved spinning as much as the girl loved the prince and so everyone was happy.

ld Mother Twitchett has but one eye,
And a long tail which she can let fly,
And every time she goes over a gap,
She leaves a bit of her tail in a trap.

The north wind doth blow,
And we shall have snow,
And what will poor robin do then?
Poor thing.
He'll sit in a barn,
And keep himself warm,
And hide his head under his wing.
Poor thing.

Six little mice sat down to spin;
Pussy passed by and she peeped in.
What are you doing, my little men?
Weaving coats for gentlemen.
Shall I come in and cut off your threads?
No, no, Mistress Pussy, you'd bite off our heads.
Oh no, I'll not; I'll help you to spin.
That may be so, but you don't come in.

Simple Simon met a pieman,
Going to the fair;
Says Simple Simon to the pieman,
Let me taste your ware.

Says the pieman to Simple Simon,
Show me first your penny;
Says Simple Simon to the pieman
Indeed I have not any.

Simple Simon went a-fishing,
For to catch a whale;
All the water he had got
Was in his mother's pail.

Simple Simon went to look
If plums grew on a thistle;
He pricked his fingers very much,
Which made poor Simon whistle.

He went for water in a sieve
But soon it all fell through;
And now poor Simple Simon
Bids you all adieu.

I saw three ships come sailing by,
Come sailing by, come sailing by,
I saw three ships come sailing by,
On New-Year's day in the morning.

And what do you think was in them then,
Was in them then, was in them then?
And what do you think was in them then,
On New-Year's day in the morning?

Three pretty girls were in them then,
Were in them then, were in them then,
Three pretty girls were in them then,
On New-Year's day in the morning.

One could whistle, and one could sing,
And one could play on the violin;
Such joy there was at my wedding,
On New-Year's day in the morning.

As I walked by myself,
And talked to myself,
Myself said unto me,
Look to thyself,
Take care of thyself,
For nobody cares for thee.

I answered myself,
And said to myself,
In the self-same repartee,
Look to thyself,
Or not to thyself,
The self-same thing will be.

I had a little husband,
No bigger than my thumb;
I put him in a pint-pot
And there I bade him drum.
I bought a little horse
That galloped up and down;
I bridled him, and saddled him
And sent him out of town.
I gave him some garters
To garter up his hose,
And a little silk handkerchief
To wipe his pretty nose.

125

ome, let's to bed,
Says Sleepy-head;
Tarry a while, says Slow;
Put on the pot,
Says Greedy-gut,
We'll sup before we go.

The White Dove

Once, on a cold and blustery day, a coach was travelling through the forest. It was bumping along over the ruts and through the puddles when a band of robbers ran from the trees.

"Your money or your lives!" they shouted.

As the coachman pulled hard on the reins, and the coach came to a halt, one of the doors jolted open. A slim girl, with brown hair, managed to slip unnoticed through the door and into the trees. She ran deeper and deeper into the forest, catching her dress on brambles and losing her shoes as she went. She did not stop running until the shouts of the robbers had faded away into the distance and all she could hear were the birds. And then, she sat on a fallen log, and buried her face in her hands. She was safe from the robbers it was true, but she was alone in a deep dark wood, with nowhere to go, and no one to help her.

"Oh woe is me," she sobbed. "What shall I do? I will never find my way out of the forest."

Presently, through her sobs, she heard the gentle whirr of wings. She looked up and saw a white dove hovering in front of her. It was carrying a tiny key in its beak. It dropped the key on the moss at her feet, and said,

''In the tree behind you, you will find a tiny lock. Open it with the key.''

Sure enough, hidden in the bark of the tree, and so tiny that she almost missed it, was a tiny keyhole. She turned the key in it and a door opened to reveal a cupboard containing bread, and milk.

''Thank you little dove,'' said the girl, through her tears.

When she had eaten, the dove dropped a second key at her feet. That opened a tree door which led to a room just large enough to hold a bed.

''Sleep there, and you will be safe,'' said the dove.

The days passed, and whenever the girl was in need of anything the dove came to her with a key which opened yet another door in yet another tree. One day, when the dove was sitting on her hand, it said, "Will you do something for me?"

"Gladly," said the girl, stroking the dove's soft feathers.

"Then listen carefully," said the dove. "Follow the path that leads into the deepest part of the wood. It will lead you to a cottage. In the cottage you will see an old woman sitting by the fire. Do not speak to her but pass on her right side and enter the room behind her. On the table you will see many rings encrusted with jewels that sparkle like fire, and amongst them, one made of gold. Please bring me the gold ring."

The girl followed the path and found the cottage. She could see the old woman sitting by the fire.

"What are you doing?" croaked the old woman, as the girl crept past her. The girl put her hand over her mouth so that she would not be tricked into speaking. She found the table covered with jewelled rings, but of the golden ring there was no sign. And then she saw the old woman sneaking through the door with a bird-cage hidden under her shawl.

'The ring must be in the cage' thought the girl, and snatched it from the old woman. Sure enough, the bird was holding the ring in its beak. The girl took it gently, and then ran to the tree where her friend the dove had told her to wait. The dove was not there. She waited, and waited, and still the dove did not come. She leant sadly against the tree, and her tears began to fall as she thought perhaps she would never see the dove again. And then, something very strange happened. The tree felt strangely soft, for a tree . . . and then, it seemed to grow arms which wrapped themselves around her.

''Do not cry,'' said a gentle voice.

The tree was changing into a prince, and all around her other trees were changing into the prince's friends.

''Do not be afraid,'' said the Prince, for of course, the girl WAS afraid. ''The woman in the cottage is a witch. She cast a spell on us all. She turned us into trees, but because I am a prince she allowed me to fly as a dove, for two hours every day.''

He gently uncurled the girl's fingers and took the ring from her hand. ''When you took this from the witch you broke her spell.''

And then the girl recognized the voice of her dear friend the dove, and she was afraid no longer.

Like most fairy stories, this one has a happy ending too. The girl married the prince and became a princess, and they lived happily ever after.

ussy cat, pussy cat, where have you been?
I've been to London to look at the queen.
Pussy cat, pussy cat, what did you there?
I frightened a little mouse under her chair.

ee Willie Winkie runs through the town,
Upstairs and downstairs in his night-gown,
Rapping at the window, crying through the lock,
Are the children all in bed, for now it's eight o'clock?

Ride a cock-horse to Banbury Cross,
To see a fine lady upon a white horse;
Rings on her fingers and bells on her toes,
And she shall have music wherever she goes.

131

Gregory Griggs, Gregory Griggs,
Had twenty seven different wigs.
He wore them up, he wore them down,
To please the people of the town;
He wore them east, he wore them west,
But he never could tell which he loved the best.

ranges and lemons,
Say the bells of St. Clement's.

You owe me five farthings,
Say the bells of St. Martin's.

When will you pay me?
Say the bells of Old Bailey.

When I grow rich,
Say the bells of Shoreditch.

When will that be?
Say the bells of Stepney.

I'm sure I don't know,
Says the great bell at Bow.

Here comes a candle to light you to bed,
Here comes a chopper to chop off your head.

B oys and girls come out to play,
The moon doth shine as bright as day.
   Leave your supper and leave your sleep,
And join your playfellows in the street.
   Come with a whoop and come with a call,
Come with a good will or not at all.
   Up the ladder and down the wall,
A half-penny loaf will serve us all;
   You find milk, and I'll find flour,
And we'll have a pudding in half an hour.

The Queen of Hearts
She made some tarts,
All on a summer's day;
The Knave of Hearts
He stole the tarts,
And took them clean away.

The King of Hearts
Called for the tarts,
And beat the knave full sore;
The Knave of Hearts
Brought back the tarts,
And vowed he'd steal no more.

135

Where are you going to, my pretty maid?
I'm going a-milking, sir, she said,
Sir, she said, sir, she said,
I'm going a-milking, sir, she said.

May I go with you, my pretty maid?
You're kindly welcome, sir, she said,
Sir, she said, sir, she said,
You're kindly welcome, sir, she said.

Say, will you marry me, my pretty maid?
Yes, if you please, kind sir, she said,
Sir, she said, sir, she said,
Yes, if you please, kind sir, she said.

What is your father, my pretty maid?
My father's a farmer, sir, she said,
Sir, she said, sir, she said,
My father's a farmer, sir, she said.

What is your fortune, my pretty maid?
My face is my fortune, sir, she said,
Sir, she said, sir, she said,
My face is my fortune, sir, she said.

Then I can't marry you, my pretty maid.
Nobody asked you, sir, she said,
Sir, she said, sir, she said,
Nobody asked you, sir, she said.

Ring-a-ring o' roses,
A pocket full of posies,
A-tishoo! A-tishoo!
We all fall down.

ittle Miss Muffet
Sat on a tuffet,
Eating her curds and whey;
There came a big spider,
Who sat down beside her
And frightened Miss Muffet away.

If all the world were paper,
And all the sea were ink,
If all the trees were bread and cheese,
What should we have to drink?

139

I had a little moppet,
I kept it in my pocket
And fed it on corn and hay;
Then came a proud beggar
And said he would wed her,
And stole my little moppet away.

I had a little hen,
The prettiest ever seen;
She washed up the dishes,
And kept the house clean.
She went to the mill
To fetch me some flour,
And always got home
In less than an hour.
She baked me my bread,
She brewed me my ale,
She sat by the fire
And told a fine tale.

Bell horses, bell horses,
What time of day?
One o'clock, two o'clock,
Time to away.

A man in the wilderness asked me,
How many strawberries grow in the sea?
I answered him, as I thought good,
As many as red herrings grow in the wood.

Aladdin

Once upon a time, there was a magician, who went to China to find a magic lamp he had heard about. He knew it was hidden in an underground cave, and he knew that the only way to get into the cave was through a narrow passage. He knew too, that if the clothes of anyone passing through the passage touched the walls, they would die. He didn't want to risk his own life, even for a magic lamp, so he befriended a Chinese boy called Aladdin, and sent him into the cave.

"Wear this ring," said the magician as Aladdin got ready to climb down into the passage. "It may help to protect you."

"Protect me? Protect me from what?" asked Aladdin.

"Nothing," said the magician quickly. "There is nothing at all to be afraid of. Down you go, there's a good lad, and bring me the little lamp which you will find on the ledge at the back of the cave."

The magician was nervous, and Aladdin seemed to be in the cave a very long time. He was just beginning to think Aladdin's clothes HAD touched the walls of the passage, and that he would never see him again, when he saw Aladdin's face framed in the gloom at the end of the passage.

"Have you got it? Give it to me!" said the magician eagerly. "Give me the lamp!" He reached down, and would have snatched the lamp from Aladdin, but Aladdin put it in his sleeve and the magician could not reach it. Aladdin had a feeling that perhaps the magician was not to be trusted, so he said,

"Help me out first, then I will give you the lamp."

"Give me the lamp first," said the magician.

"Help me out first," said Aladdin. The magician wouldn't give in, and neither would Aladdin. Suddenly, the magician lost his patience and his temper.

"If you will not give me the lamp, then you can stay in the cave for EVER!" he shouted, and he closed the entrance to the passage with a short, sharp spell, and went away fuming.

Poor Aladdin! He didn't know what to do. He sat in the dark and tried to think. Then he absent-mindedly rubbed the ring which the magician had given him before he went into the cave. There was a hiss and a strange wispy figure, wearing a turban, curled up in the air in front of him like smoke from a fire. Aladdin gasped, and shielded his eyes from the sudden light.

"Who . . . who are you?" he asked.

"I am the genie of the ring. What is your command oh master?"

"Can you take me home?" asked Aladdin.

Before Aladdin had time to blink he found himself standing outside his own house, wondering if he was asleep or awake. He knew he couldn't be dreaming when he found the lamp tucked inside his sleeve. He took it to his mother.

"We can sell this and buy food," he said.

"No one will buy a dusty old lamp," said Aladdin's mother. "Let me clean it first." She had rubbed it but once, when there was a hiss, and another strange figure appeared and wavered in the air like a wisp of smoke. Aladdin's mother was very frightened, but Aladdin asked,

"Who are you?"

"I am the genie of the lamp. What is your command oh master?"

And that's how it came about that Aladdin and his mother became rich. Whatever they wanted the genie of the lamp provided, and when Aladdin fell in love with a princess he was rich enough to marry her and take her to live in a beautiful palace.

Aladdin and his princess lived happily for a long time. They shared all their secrets, except one. Aladdin never told the princess about the magic lamp.

One day, when Aladdin was out hunting, and the princess was at home in the palace, an old pedlar called from the street, "New lamps for old! New lamps for old!"

Now, though Aladdin had never spoken about the lamp to his princess, she had seen it, and when she heard the calls of the pedlar, who was really the wicked magician in disguise, she thought, 'I will get Aladdin a new lamp'. She ran into the street and exchanged, what she thought was a useless and broken lamp, for a bright and shining new one.

Immediately he had the magic lamp in his hand, the magician dropped the basket and threw off his disguise.

"He . . . he . . . he . . ." he chortled. "Now everything Aladdin has shall be mine." He summoned the genie of the lamp and ordered him to take him, Aladdin's palace and Aladdin's princess to far away Africa.

When Aladdin returned home there was nothing but dust and a bare patch where the palace had been. He guessed at once that the magician was responsible. He quickly summoned the genie of the ring.

"What is your command oh master?" asked the genie.

"Please bring back my princess and my palace," said Aladdin.

"I cannot. Only the genie of the lamp can do that."

"Then take me to my princess, wherever she may be," commanded Aladdin.

That, the genie of the ring could do. And he did so. The princess was overjoyed to see Aladdin.

"I've come to take you home," said Aladdin. "But first we must outwit the magician and retrieve the lamp. Slip this powder into his wine when he is not looking."

The powder made the magician sleep, and while he slept Aladdin was able to take the lamp from his pocket.

Aladdin summoned the genie of the lamp.

"What is your command oh master?" asked the genie.

"Leave the magician here in the middle of Africa, and take the palace, and everyone else in it, back to China," said Aladdin.

And that is what the genie of the lamp did. And everyone, except the magician, who woke up and found himself on a sand dune and who is still trying to work out how he got there, lived happily ever after.

ittle Boy Blue,
Come blow your horn,
The sheep's in the meadow,
The cow's in the corn;
But where is the boy
Who looks after the sheep?
He's under a haystack,
Fast asleep.
Will you wake him?
No, not I,
For if I do,
He's sure to cry.

Mr Ibister, and Betsy his sister,
Resolved upon giving a treat;
So letters they write,
Their friends to invite,
To their house in Great Camomile Street.

Tom, Tom, the piper's son,
Stole a pig and away he run;
The pig was eat
And Tom was beat,
And Tom went howling down the street.

London Bridge is broken down,
Broken down, broken down,
London Bridge is broken down,
My fair lady.

Build it up with wood and clay,
Wood and clay, wood and clay,
Build it up with wood and clay,
My fair lady.

Wood and clay will wash away,
Wash away, wash away,
Wood and clay will wash away,
My fair lady.

Build it up with bricks and mortar,
Bricks and mortar, bricks and mortar,
Build it up with bricks and mortar,
My fair lady.

Bricks and mortar will not stay,
Will not stay, will not stay,
Bricks and mortar will not stay,
My fair lady.

Build it up with iron and steel,
Iron and steel, iron and steel,
Build it up with iron and steel,
My fair lady.

Iron and steel will bend and bow,
Bend and bow, bend and bow,
Iron and steel will bend and bow,
My fair lady.

Build it up with silver and gold,
Silver and gold, silver and gold,
Build it up with silver and gold,
My fair lady.

Silver and gold will be stolen away,
Stolen away, stolen away,
Silver and gold will be stolen away,
My fair lady.

Set a man to watch all night,
Watch all night, watch all night,
Set a man to watch all night,
My fair lady.

Suppose the man should fall asleep,
Fall asleep, fall asleep,
Suppose the man should fall asleep?
My fair lady.

Give him a pipe to smoke all night,
Smoke all night, smoke all night,
Give him a pipe to smoke all night,
My fair lady.

What are little boys made of?
What are little boys made of?
Frogs and snails
And puppy-dogs' tails,
That's what little boys are made of.

What are little girls made of?
What are little girls made of?
Sugar and spice
And all that's nice,
That's what little girls are made of.

Cross-patch,
Draw the latch,
Sit by the fire and spin;
Take a cup,
And drink it up,
Then call your neighbours in.

Little Jack Horner
Sat in the corner,
Eating a Christmas pie;
He put in his thumb,
And pulled out a plum,
And said, What a good boy am I!

 Baa, baa, black sheep,
Have you any wool?
Yes, sir, yes, sir,
Three bags full;
One for the master,
And one for the dame,
And one for the little boy
Who lives down the lane.

Jorinda and Joringel

Once upon a time, there was a witch who lived in a castle in the middle of a dark and tangled wood. At night she read her magic books, but by day she changed herself into an owl and flew about the wood, ready to cast a spell on anyone who dared to get too close to her castle.

One day a boy and girl were walking in the wood. They had a wedding to plan and a lot to talk about, and they went deeper into the wood than they intended. Just as the sun was about to set, Joringel said,

"We should turn for home . . . we are getting too close to the witch's castle." But it was already too late, for even as he spoke an owl flew from the trees and circled round them.

"Whoo! Whoo! Whoo!" it cried. The witch's spell had been cast. Joringel could not move and Jorinda had been turned into a little brown bird.

The owl flew into the middle of a bush. There was a rustle, and a moment later the old witch herself appeared. She caught the brown bird in a wicker cage and hurried away with it towards the castle. And though Joringel could see everything as it happened, he could do nothing to help Jorinda. He was rooted to the spot. And there he stayed, as still as a stone statue, until the old witch returned and removed the spell.

"Where is Jorinda? What have you done with her? Please bring her back to me," he begged. But the old witch was deaf to all his pleas.

"Go home . . ." she said. "Stop wasting my time."

Joringel tried again, and again, to get into the castle, but every time the witch was ready for him. Whenever he got to within a hundred paces of the grey crumbling walls, she cast her spell afresh, and he could not move. He despaired of ever seeing Jorinda again. And then one night, when he had fallen into an exhausted and fitful sleep, he had a strange dream. He dreamed that he had found a large pearl in the centre of a beautiful red flower. In his dream he picked the flower, and found that everything he touched with it was released from the witch's spell.

When Joringel woke he was determined to search until he found just such a flower. It was the only hope he had. He searched through the woods and the meadows for eight whole days, and then on the ninth day, he found a flower just like the one in his dream, except that instead of a pearl nestling inside its velvety red petals, there was a bright and glistening dew-drop. Joringel picked it carefully so that he did not disturb the dew-drop, then cradled it gently in his hands and hurried towards the castle.

"If only everything happens as it did in my dream," he whispered when he got as far as the castle door without being stopped. He had never got so close to the castle before. He touched the door with the flower. It flew open. As he walked through the dark and cobwebby castle the witch danced round him, screeching and shouting, and casting all the spells she could think of and making up lots of new ones too. But nothing worked. The flower's magic was stronger than hers.

Presently, Joringel came to a room where seven hundred wicker cages hung from hooks in the ceiling. Sitting forlornly in each cage was a sad brown bird.

Out of seven hundred, how could he tell which was Jorinda? And then Joringel saw the witch sneaking away with one of the cages hidden in the crook of her arm. He knew at once that THAT was Jorinda. He snatched the cage from the witch and opened the door. The instant the velvety red petals of the flower brushed against the bird's wing it turned back into Jorinda.

"I knew you would come," she whispered. "I knew you would find a way of rescuing me."

Now that he had found Jorinda, Joringel set about freeing all the other little brown birds from the witch's spell. Soon there were seven hundred empty cages swinging from the ceiling.

From that day onwards, the witch lost her power to cast spells and it was safe to walk anywhere in the wood, by day, or by night.

Tweedledum and Tweedledee
Agreed to have a battle,
For Tweedledum said Tweedledee
Had spoiled his nice new rattle.
Just then flew by a monstrous crow,
As big as a tar-barrel,
Which frightened both the heroes so,
They quite forgot their quarrel.

Jack Sprat could eat no fat,
His wife could eat no lean,
And so between them both, you see,
They licked the platter clean.

Pease porridge hot,
Pease porridge cold,
Pease porridge in the pot
Nine days old.

Some like it hot,
Some like it cold,
Some like it in the pot
Nine days old.

ing, sing, what shall I sing?
The cat's run away with the pudding-string!
Do, do, what shall I do?
The cat has bitten it quite in two.

had a little nut tree,
Nothing would it bear
But a silver nutmeg
And a golden pear;

The King of Spain's daughter
Came to visit me,
And all for the sake
Of my little nut tree.

168

Lavender's blue, diddle, diddle,
Lavender's green;
When I am king, diddle, diddle,
You shall be queen.

Call up your men, diddle, diddle,
Set them to work,
Some to the plough, diddle, diddle,
Some to the cart.

Some to make hay, diddle, diddle,
Some to thresh corn,
Whilst you and I, diddle, diddle,
Keep ourselves warm.

Solomon Grundy,
Born on a Monday,
Christened on Tuesday,
Married on Wednesday,
Took ill on Thursday,
Worse on Friday,
Died on Saturday,
Buried on Sunday.
This is the end
Of Solomon Grundy.

If I had a donkey that wouldn't go,
Would I beat him? Oh no, no.
I'd put him in the barn and give him some corn,
The best little donkey that ever was born.

Puss in Boots

Once upon a time, there was a miller, who had three sons. When he died he left his mill to his first son, his donkey to his second son, and because he had nothing else, he left his cat to his third son.

The first son ground flour at the mill and sold it. The second son harnessed the donkey to a cart and carried things for paying customers. But what could the third son do with a cat, except let him sit in the sun, and purr, and drink milk?

One day, the cat said, "Master, give me a pair of boots and a sack and you will see that I am not as useless as you think." It was a very strange request for a cat to make, but it was granted nonetheless.

The cat, or Puss in Boots, as the miller's son now called him, went into the forest and caught a rabbit. He put it in the sack and then instead of taking it home to the miller's son, he took it to the King's palace.

"Please accept this small present from my master the Marquis of Carabas," said Puss in Boots.

It was to be the first of many presents Puss in Boots took to the King, and each time he said he had been sent by his master the Marquis of Carabas. And though the King never actually met the Marquis of Carabas, he soon became very familiar with his name. The miller's son knew nothing of the presents, or of the Marquis of Carabas, and Puss in Boots didn't tell him.

One day, when Puss in Boots was at the palace, he overheard someone say that the King was about to take his daughter for a drive in the country. Puss in Boots hurried home.

"Quick master!" he called. "Go and bathe in the river and I will make your fortune."

It was another strange request for a cat to make but the miller's son was used to his pet by now and so he did as he was told. No sooner was he in the river than Puss in Boots took his clothes and threw them into the river with him.

"Puss . . . Puss . . . what are you doing?" called the miller's son.

Puss didn't answer, he was watching the road. Presently he saw the King's carriage in the distance. He waited until it was close then he ran out in the road in front of it.

"Help! Help! My master the Marquis of Carabas is drowning! Please save him!"

It took but a moment to drag the miller's son, who hadn't the slightest idea what Puss in Boots was up to, from the river and find him some dry clothes. He looked so handsome in the fine velvet tunic and the doublet and hose borrowed from one of the footmen that the princess fell in love with him at once.

"Father dear, may the Marquis of Carabas ride with us?"

The King liked to please his daughter and agreed to her request at once.

"Will you ride with us Puss?" asked the King.

Puss asked to be excused. He said he had something rather important to attend to. He ran on ahead of the carriage, and each time he saw someone at work in the fields he called,

"If the King asks who this land belongs to, tell him it belongs to the Marquis of Carabas."

The King did stop the carriage several times, and each time he received the same answer to his question.

'The Marquis of Carabas must be a very rich man,' he thought.

Puss in Boots ran so swiftly that soon he was a long way ahead of the carriage. Presently he came to a rich and imposing looking castle, which he knew belonged to a cruel and wicked ogre. He went straight up to the ogre without so much as a twitching of a whisker, and said,

"I hear you can turn yourself into any animal you choose. I won't believe a story like that unless I see it for myself."

Immediately, the ogre changed himself into a lion, and roared and growled and snarled.

"There . . ." he said, when he had turned himself back into an ogre. "I hope I frightened you."

"Must be easy to change your- self into something big," said Puss in Boots with a shrug. "I don't suppose you can turn your- self into something as small as a . . . er . . . um . . ." He seemed to be thinking. " . . . er . . . um . . . a mouse?"

The ogre couldn't have a mere cat doubting his special abilities. He changed himself into a tiny mouse in the twinkling of an eye. It was the last time he changed himself into anything because Puss in Boots pounced on him and ate him up before he could change back into an ogre, and THAT was the end of him!

"Hoorah!" shouted the castle servants. "We are free of the wicked ogre at last. Hoorah!"

"Your new master will always be kind, you can be sure of that," said Puss in Boots.

"Who IS our new master?" they asked.

"The Marquis of Carabas of course," said Puss.

When the King's carriage reached the castle, Puss in Boots was standing at the drawbridge, with the smiling servants gathered round him.

"Welcome . . " he said with a beautiful bow. "Welcome to the home of my master the Marquis of Carabas." The miller's son was too astonished to do anything except think to himself,

'Whatever is Puss up to?'

Luckily Puss had time to explain while the King was getting out of the carriage.

'What a rich man this Marquis must be,' thought the King. 'And such a nice young man too.'

Not long afterwards the princess and the miller's son were married. They, and Puss in Boots, lived happily ever after in the castle that had once belonged to the wicked ogre.

s a little fat man of Bombay
Was smoking one very hot day,
A bird called a snipe
Flew away with his pipe,
Which vexed the fat man of Bombay.

ack be nimble,
Jack be quick,
Jack jump over
The candle stick.

177

at-a-cake, pat-a-cake, baker's man,
Bake me a cake as fast as you can;
Pat it and prick it, and mark it with B,
Put it in the oven for baby and me.

The first day of Christmas,
My true love sent to me
A partridge in a pear tree.

The second day of Christmas,
My true love sent to me
Two turtle doves, and
A partridge in a pear tree.

The third day of Christmas,
My true love sent to me
Three French hens,
Two turtle doves, and
A partridge in a pear tree.

The fourth day of Christmas,
My true love sent to me
Four colly birds,
Three French hens,
Two turtle doves, and
A partridge in a pear tree.

The fifth day of Christmas,
My true love sent to me
Five gold rings,
Four colly birds,
Three French hens,
Two turtle doves, and
A partridge in a pear tree.

179

The sixth day of Christmas,
My true love sent to me
Six geese a-laying,
Five gold rings,
Four colly birds,
Three French hens,
Two turtle doves, and
A partridge in a pear tree.

The seventh day of Christmas,
My true love sent to me
Seven swans a-swimming,
Six geese a-laying,
Five gold rings,
Four colly birds,
Three French hens,
Two turtle doves, and
A partridge in a pear tree.

The eighth day of Christmas,
My true love sent to me
Eight maids a-milking,
Seven swans a-swimming,
Six geese a-laying,
Five gold rings,
Four colly birds,
Three French hens,
Two turtle doves, and
A partridge in a pear tree.

The ninth day of Christmas,
My true love sent to me
Nine drummers drumming,
Eight maids a-milking,
Seven swans a-swimming,
Six geese a-laying,
Five gold rings,
Four colly birds,
Three French hens,
Two turtle doves, and
A partridge in a pear tree.

The tenth day of Christmas,
My true love sent to me
Ten pipers piping,
Nine drummers drumming,
Eight maids a-milking,
Seven swans a-swimming,
Six geese a-laying,
Five gold rings,
Four colly birds,
Three French hens,
Two turtle doves, and
A partridge in a pear tree.

181

The eleventh day of Christmas,
My true love sent to me
Eleven ladies dancing,
Ten pipers piping,
Nine drummers drumming,
Eight maids a-milking,
Seven swans a-swimming,
Six geese a-laying,
Five gold rings,
Four colly birds,
Three French hens,
Two turtle doves, and
A partridge in a pear tree.

The twelfth day of Christmas,
My true love sent to me
Twelve lords a-leaping,
Eleven ladies dancing,
Ten pipers piping,
Nine drummers drumming,
Eight maids a-milking,
Seven swans a-swimming,
Six geese a-laying,
Five gold rings,
Four colly birds,
Three French hens,
Two turtle doves, and
A partridge in a pear tree.

Polly put the kettle on,
Polly put the kettle on,
Polly put the kettle on,
We'll all have tea.

Sukey take it off again,
Sukey take it off again,
Sukey take it off again,
They've all gone away.

Gray goose and gander,
Waft your wings together
And carry the good king's daughter
Over the one-strand river.

ld King Cole
Was a merry old soul,
And a merry old soul was he;
He called for his pipe,
And he called for his bowl,
And he called for his fiddlers three.

Every fiddler, he had a fiddle,
And a very fine fiddle had he;
Twee tweedle dee, tweedle dee, went the fiddlers.
Oh, there's none so rare
As can compare
With King Cole and his fiddlers three.

ittle Bob Robin,
Where do you live?
Up in yonder wood, sir,
On a hazel twig.

ittle Betty Blue
Lost her holiday shoe,
What can little Betty do?
Give her another
To match the other,
And then she may walk out in two.

The Brave Little Tailor

One day, a tailor was sitting at his bench sewing a seam with his needle and thread. Beside him was a plate and on the plate was a slice of bread and jam. It was his lunch and the sooner he finished sewing the seam the sooner he could eat it. He liked jam spread on bread. He wasn't the only one.

"Jam . . ." buzzed the greedy flies. "We smell jam."

"Don't you dare!" shouted the little tailor. He picked up a piece of cloth. "Take that!" he shouted, and he swatted at the flies as hard as he could. Seven of them fell dead to the table.

"How clever I am!" said the little tailor proudly. "I have killed seven with one blow. I must tell the world about this." And so that the whole world could see at a glance how clever he was he made himself a belt, and on the belt he embroidered the words SEVEN WITH ONE BLOW.

He put some cheese in his pocket in case he got hungry and then he set off. Beside the door, as he went out, was a small brown bird caught in a bush. He untangled it from the prickly briars and put it in his pocket with the cheese.

He followed a road that wound round the side of a mountain like a corkscrew. At the fourth turn in the road he met a giant carrying a tree.

"Would you like to walk with me and keep me company?" called the brave little tailor.

"Ho .. ho .." laughed the giant who was as tall as a tree himself. The brave little tailor barely reached his knee. "Ho .. ho .. ME walk with YOU . . . ho .. ho .. ho .."

"Read that!" said the brave little tailor, pointing to his belt. "And then see if you feel like laughing."

"SEVEN WITH ONE BLOW" read the giant. He thought that meant the brave little tailor had killed seven ogres . . . or seven dragons . . . or maybe seven knights in armour . . . and he was very impressed. Nonetheless, he decided to test the brave little tailor. After all, it is easy enough to SAY you are brave and strong. He picked up a rock that would have squashed the brave little tailor had it fallen on him.

"Can YOU do this?" asked the giant. He squeezed the rock until the perspiration stood in beads on his brow, and finally a tiny trickle of water ran from it.

"That's easy enough," said the brave little tailor. He put his hand into his pocket and took out the cheese. It was soft squashy cheese. One tiny squeeze and the whey ran between his fingers in a milky stream.

189

"Oh!" said the giant, rather taken aback. Then he said, "Can YOU throw as far as this?" He picked up a small boulder and hurled it with all his might. It flew through the air like a thunderbolt and landed with a thud on the grass, at least half a league away.

"Easily," said the brave little tailor. This time he took the little brown bird from his pocket. It had got over its fright at being tangled in the briar and was glad to be free. When the brave little tailor tossed it into the air, it flew and flew until it was just a tiny speck in the distance.

"It will fall to the ground sooner or later," said the brave little tailor. "Probably later, rather than sooner."

"If you're THAT strong," said the giant, feeling more than a little put out, "you can help me carry this tree home."

"Glad to," said the brave little tailor. "You go in front and take the roots, I'll follow behind and carry the branches, which are the heaviest part."

The giant lifted the heavy trunk back onto his shoulder. The knobbly roots stuck out in front of him like a lopsided beard and he didn't see the brave little tailor leap nimbly into the branches behind him and settle himself comfortably.

"Ready when you are!" called the brave little tailor.

He rode all the way to the giant's cave. His feet didn't touch the ground once. When they got to the cave the giant lowered the tree to the ground and sat down himself. He didn't see the brave little tailor jump to the ground. The brave little tailor wasn't the slightest bit out of breath. He didn't look the slightest bit tired. The giant couldn't believe his eyes. HE was tired. HE was out of breath. And he was frightened as well. If the brave little tailor was as strong as he seemed to be then he could be dangerous, even to a giant. He would have to be got rid of.

"Come to the cave and meet my brothers," said the giant slyly. "You can spend the night with us."

That night, the giant let the brave little tailor sleep in his own bed, while he slept on the floor. The bed was just the right size, and comfortable for a giant, but for the brave little tailor it was too big and far too uncomfortable. Each lump in the mattress felt like a small mountain. He could not sleep at all and at last he crawled into a corner and fell asleep there. And what a good thing he did, for in the night, the giant smote the bed with an iron bar. If the brave little tailor had been sleeping in it he would surely have been killed.

The next morning the giants were having breakfast, happy in the thought that the brave little tailor who had killed seven with one blow, was now dead himself. They had the surprise of their lives when the brave little tailor called for his breakfast.

They bellowed with fright and
ran from the cave. They ran
until they came to the sea and
they splashed through that until
they reached the land on the far
side. They are probably running
still. The brave little tailor
puffed out his chest when he
saw the three giants running away
from HIM. He felt brave enough
to conquer a hundred giants.

He tricked a lot of people
into believing he was stronger
than he really was. Even kings
trembled at the thought of what
he might do. One day he became
a king himself, but that is a
story for another time.

o market, to market, to buy a fat pig,
Home again, home again, jiggety-jig;
To market, to market, to buy a fat hog,
Home again, home again, jiggety-jog.

Three young rats with black felt hats,
Three young ducks with white straw flats,
Three young dogs with curling tails,
Three young cats with demi-veils,
Went out to walk with two young pigs
In satin vests and sorrel wigs.
But suddenly it chanced to rain
And so they all went home again.

Sing a song of sixpence,
A pocket full of rye;
Four and twenty blackbirds,
Baked in a pie.
  When the pie was opened,
  The birds began to sing;
  Was not that a dainty dish,
  To set before the king?

The king was in his counting house,
Counting out his money;
The queen was in the parlour,
Eating bread and honey.

The maid was in the garden,
Hanging out the clothes,
There came a little blackbird,
And snapped off her nose.

There was a little woman,
As I have heard tell,
She went to market
Her eggs for to sell;
She went to market
All on a market day,
And she fell asleep
On the king's highway.

There came by a pedlar,
His name was Stout,
He cut her petticoats
All round about;
He cut her petticoats
Up to her knees;
Which made the little woman
To shiver and sneeze.

When this little woman
Began to awake,
She began to shiver,
And she began to shake;
She began to shake,
And she began to cry,
Lawk a mercy on me,
This is none of I!

But if this be I,
As I do hope it be,
I have a little dog at home
And he knows me;
If it be I,
He'll wag his little tail,
And if it be not I
He'll loudly bark and wail!

Home went the little woman
All in the dark,
Up starts the little dog,
And he began to bark;
He began to bark,
And she began to cry,
Lawk a mercy on me,
This is none of I!

The cock crows in the morn
To tell us to rise,
And he that lies late
Will never be wise:
For early to bed,
And early to rise,
Is the way to be healthy
And wealthy and wise.

Dance to your daddy,
My little babby,
Dance to your daddy, my little lamb;
You shall have a fishy
In a little dishy,
You shall have a fishy when the boat comes in.

I went into my grandmother's garden,
And there I found a farthing.
I went into my next door neighbour's;
There I bought a pipkin and a popkin,
A slipkin and a slopkin,
A nailboard, a sailboard,
And all for a farthing.

Foolish Jack

Foolish Jack never stopped to think things out for himself. And sometimes, as you can well imagine, that led him into trouble.

One day his mother sent him out to work. He raked hay all day for the farmer and at the end of the day the farmer gave him a penny. Jack tied the penny in his handkerchief, but somewhere on the way home, he lost the handkerchief and the penny.

"You silly boy!" said his mother. "You should have put it in your pocket."

Next day Jack went to work at the dairy. When evening came the dairyman gave him a jug of milk.

Jack did not want to lose the milk as he had lost the penny, so he put the jug in his pocket. He had to tip it on its side to get it in, and of course it spilt. What a mess it made.

"You silly boy!" said his mother, when he got home. "You should have carried it on your head."

The following day Jack helped the man who kept hens. He gave Jack six brown eggs to take home.

"I know exactly what to do to keep them safe," said Jack. He ruffled his hair and balanced the eggs on his head as though he was a tree and his hair was a nest. It wasn't a very good nest and eggs having no corners to stop them rolling, it wasn't long before they rolled off Jack's head and onto the ground.

"You silly boy!" said his mother, when he got home. "You should have carried them in your hands."

Next day Jack was given a roly-poly piglet. If you have ever tried to carry a roly-poly piglet you will know that Jack didn't get very far before the piglet had struggled free and run away.

"You silly boy!" said his mother, when he got home. "You should have led it home on a string."

Jack was determined not to lose any more wages. When the butcher gave him a joint of meat for his labours he tied a string round THAT and led THAT home behind him. What the dogs and cats didn't snatch was covered in dust.

"You silly boy!" said his mother, stamping her foot crossly. "You should have carried it on your shoulder." She was so cross she sent him to bed without any supper.

And then Jack's luck changed, though it didn't seem like it to begin with. He had worked all day for the goatherd and had been given a goat to take home.

Now it so happened that on the way home every day Jack had to pass the house of a rich man. The rich man had a beautiful daughter who had never laughed, and he promised that the first person to make her laugh should marry her.

She had watched Jack go by the house every day. When she saw him trying to carry eggs on his head, her eyes had twinkled. When she saw him trying to carry a roly-poly piglet she had smiled, just a little. On the day he came past the house with a protesting goat wrapped round his neck like a scarf and with his own knees buckling beneath him, she burst into merry peals of laughter.

And that was how Jack found a wife. She was as sensible as she was rich, and she taught Jack how to think for himself, and so they lived happily ever after.

Brow bender,
Eye peeper,
Nose dreeper,
Mouth eater,
Chin chopper,
Knock at the door,
Ring the bell,
Lift up the latch,
Walk in . . .
Take a chair,
Sit by there,
How d'you do this morning?

As I was going to St. Ives,
I met a man with seven wives,
Each wife had seven sacks,
Each sack had seven cats,
Each cat had seven kits:
Kits, cats, sacks, and wives,
How many were there going to St. Ives?

Goosey, goosey gander,
Whither shall I wander?
Upstairs and downstairs
And in my lady's chamber.
There I met an old man
Who would not say his prayers.
I took him by the left leg
And threw him down the stairs.

There was a king, and he had three daughters,
And they all lived in a basin of water;
The basin bended,
My story's ended.
If the basin had been stronger,
My story would have been longer.

Old chairs to mend! Old chairs to mend!
I never would cry old chairs to mend,
If I'd as much money as I could spend,
I never would cry old chairs to mend.

Old clothes to sell! Old clothes to sell!
I never would cry old clothes to sell,
If I'd as much money as I could tell,
I never would cry old clothes to sell.

Hot cross buns!
Hot cross buns!
One a penny, two a penny,
Hot cross buns!
If your daughters do not like them
Give them to your sons;
But if you haven't any of these pretty little elves
You cannot do better than eat them yourselves.

209

ide a cock-horse to Banbury Cross,
To buy little Johnny a galloping horse;
It trots behind and it ambles before,
And Johnny shall ride till he can ride no more.

hree blind mice, see how they run!
They all ran after the farmer's wife,
Who cut off their tails with a carving knife,
Did you ever see such a thing in your life,
As three blind mice?

When I was a little girl,
About seven years old,
I hadn't got a petticoat,
To keep me from the cold.

So I went into Darlington,
That pretty little town,
And there I bought a petticoat,
A cloak, and a gown.

I went into the woods
And built me a kirk,
And all the birds of the air,
They helped me to work.

The hawk, with his long claws,
Pulled down the stone,
The dove, with her rough bill,
Brought me them home.

The parrot was the clergyman,
The peacock was the clerk,
The bullfinch played the organ,
And we made merry work.

If all the seas were one sea,
What a great sea that would be!
If all the trees were one tree,
What a great tree that would be!
And if all the axes were one axe,
What a great axe that would be!
And if all the men were one man,
What a great man that would be!
And if the great man took the great axe
And cut down the great tree,
And let it fall into the great sea,
What a splish-splash that would be!

The Shepherdess and the Sweep

Once there was a shepherdess. Not a real shepherdess but a delicate porcelain one. She was very beautiful. She stood beside the porcelain sweep, on a table, in a dark and crowded parlour. The sweep was as black as coal, except for his face which was as pink and as clean as the shepherdess's own. Just behind them stood the Chinese mandarin. He had a black stubby pig-tail hanging down his back, and grey slanting eyes. The Chinese mandarin nodded all the time. He couldn't help it. It was the way he was made. The shepherdess called him Grandfather, though he wasn't, because if he had been she would have been Chinese too, and she wasn't.

On the far side of the room and facing the table where the three porcelain figures stood, was a carved wooden cabinet. Carved in the very middle of the door was a very peculiar man. He had a lop-sided smile that was hardly a smile at all, and a beard, and legs like a goat. The children who lived in the house and sometimes came into the parlour called him Mr. Goat-legged, Commanding General, Private, Sergeant, because they thought it suited him, though if they were in a hurry they called him Mr. Goat-legs.

215

One day, Mr. Goat-legs asked the Chinese mandarin if he could marry the shepherdess. The Chinese mandarin nodded, as was his habit.

"Good," said Mr. Goat-legs looking pleased.

"But Grandpa, I don't want to marry horrid Mr. Goat-legs," said the shepherdess.

"It is too late now. I have given my consent," said the Chinese mandarin. "The wedding will be tonight. Wake me up in time for the ceremony." And with no more ado, he nodded himself to sleep.

The little shepherdess cried tears that looked like seed pearls. The sweep tried to comfort her.

"Please take me away from the parlour and out into the wide world," she pleaded. "I cannot marry Mr. Goat-legs."

The running stags carved on the side of the cabinet saw them climbing down to the floor.

"The shepherdess and the sweep are eloping!" they cried.

The mandarin woke with a start and began nodding so furiously, his whole body rocked backwards and forwards. The shepherdess and the sweep had never seen him so angry and were very frightened.

"There is only one way to escape," whispered the sweep. "We must go into the stove and up the chimney to the roof."

It was a difficult climb, even for the sweep. It was dark, and sooty, and steep. The shepherdess was so afraid she would slip. If she fell she knew she would break into a thousand pieces.

"Do not look down," whispered the sweep as he followed behind and guided her feet to the nooks and crannies. "Look up towards the star which shines at the end of our journey."

When the shepherdess looked up through the dark tunnel of the chimney, she could see a tiny speck of light, far, far away in the distance. The higher they climbed the bigger it grew, and when they got to the top it became the entire sky.

The shepherdess and the sweep sat side by side on the rim of the chimney-pot and looked wearily across the rooftops at the wide, wide world. The shepherdess did not like what she saw. The big wide world was so very big, and so very wide. She began to cry again.

"Please take me back to the parlour," she sobbed. "I like the big wide world even less than I like Mr. Goat-legs." Her face was soon stained with sooty tears. The little sweep could not bear to see her so unhappy and agreed to take her back.

The journey down the chimney was just as difficult as the journey up had been. It was just as dark. Just as frightening. When they finally crawled out of the stove and into the parlour they were met by a strange and eerie silence.

''Something has happened!'' cried the shepherdess. ''Oh I just know something dreadful has happened!''

It had. In his anger, the Chinese mandarin had rolled off the edge of the table and now he was lying in pieces on the floor.

''Oh dear, it's all our fault,'' cried the shepherdess. ''Oh poor Grandpa . . . what are we to do?'' And she cried even more.

''We can't do anything,'' said the sweep, ''but don't worry. Someone is sure to come along and glue him together again.''

And someone did. But from that day onwards he lost his habit of nodding. It didn't matter how many times Mr. Goat-legs asked if he could still marry the shepherdess, the Chinese mandarin, would not, could not, nod and give his consent. And so the shepherdess and the sweep were able to stand side by side until the end of their days.

Rub-a-dub-dub,
Three men in a tub,
And how do you think they got there?
The butcher, the baker,
The candlestick-maker,
They all jumped out of a rotten potato,
'Twas enough to make a man stare.

One misty, moisty, morning,
When cloudy was the weather,
There I met an old man
Clothed all in leather;
Clothed all in leather,
With cap under his chin.
How do you do, and how do you do,
And how do you do again?

219

There was an old woman of Surrey,
Who was morn, noon, and night in a hurry;
Called her husband a fool,
Drove her children to school,
The worrying old woman of Surrey.

randfa' Grig
Had a pig,
In a field of clover;
Piggie died,
Grandfa' cried,
And all the fun was over.

ow, wow, wow,
Whose dog art thou?
Little Tom Tinker's dog,
Bow, wow, wow.

The lion and the unicorn
Were fighting for the crown;
The lion beat the unicorn
All round about the town.

Some gave them white bread,
And some gave them brown;
Some gave them plum cake
And drummed them out of town.

223

*T*wo little dicky birds,
Sitting on a wall;
One named Peter,
The other named Paul.

Fly away, Peter!
Fly away, Paul!

Come back, Peter!
Come back, Paul!

Monday's child is fair of face,

Tuesday's child is full of grace,

Wednesday's child is full of woe,

Thursday's child has far to go,

Friday's child is loving and giving,

Saturday's child works hard for his living,

And the child that is born on the Sabbath day
Is bonny and blithe, and good and gay.

Ding, dong, bell,
Pussy's in the well.
Who put her in?
Little Johnny Green.
Who pulled her out?
Little Tommy Stout.
What a naughty boy was that,
To try to drown poor pussy cat,
Who never did him any harm,
And killed the mice in his father's barn.

ack and Jill went up the hill
To fetch a pail of water;
Jack fell down and broke his crown,
And Jill came tumbling after.

Up Jack got, and home did trot,
As fast as he could caper,
To old Dame Dob, who patched his nob
With vinegar and brown paper.

Twinkle, twinkle, little star,
How I wonder what you are!
Up above the world so high,
Like a diamond in the sky.

When the blazing sun is gone,
When he nothing shines upon,
Then you show your little light,
Twinkle, twinkle, all the night.

Then the traveller in the dark,
Thanks you for your tiny spark,
He could not see which way to go,
If you did not twinkle so.

In the dark blue sky you keep,
And often through my curtains peep,
For you never shut your eye,
'Till the sun is in the sky.

As your bright and tiny spark,
Lights the traveller in the dark,
Though I know not what you are,
Twinkle, twinkle, little star.

There was an old woman tossed up in a basket,
Seventeen times as high as the moon;
  Where she was going I couldn't but ask it,
  For in her hand she carried a broom.
  Old woman, old woman, old woman, quoth I,
  Where are you going to up so high?
  To brush the cobwebs off the sky!
  May I go with you?
  Aye, by-and-by.

The Ugly Duckling

Once, somewhere in the country, there was a duck who had a clutch of eggs to hatch. Five of them hatched into fluffy little ducklings, but the sixth, which for some reason was bigger than all the others, lay in the nest, smooth and unbroken.

"That's much too big to be a duck egg," said one of the duck's friends. "Looks more like a turkey egg to me."

"How will I be able to tell?" asked the duck.

"It will not swim when it is hatched," said her friend. "Turkeys never do."

But the egg wasn't a turkey egg because the bird that hatched from it DID swim. It swam as well as any duckling.

"That last duckling of yours is very ugly," laughed the farmyard hens. It was true. He wasn't a bit like his brothers and sisters.

"What an ugly duckling," laughed the geese when they saw him. And somehow that name stuck. Whenever anyone wanted him they called, "Ugly duckling, where are you?" or if they didn't want him they said, "Ugly duckling, go away." He even thought of himself as ugly duckling. He was very sad. He didn't like being ugly. He didn't like being teased. No one would play with him. No one would swim with him. Even his mother made fun of him. One day, the ugly duckling ran away. And I am sorry to say, no one missed him at all.

The ugly duckling hoped he would find someone in the big wide world, to be his friend. Someone who wouldn't mind how ugly he was. But the wild ducks were just as unkind as the farmyard ducks, and the wild geese honked at him and made fun, just as the farmyard geese had done.

"Am I never to find a friend? Am I never to be happy?" sighed the ugly duckling.

One day, as he sat alone and unhappy in the middle of a lake on the bleak flat marshes, he heard the steady beat of wings. When he looked up there were swans flying overhead with their long necks stretched before them and their white feathers gleaming in the sun. They were so beautiful. If only he had been born a swan. But he hadn't. He had been born a duckling and an ugly one at that.

The ugly duckling stayed on the lake all through the long hard winter. Food was hard to find and he was often hungry. Once he was trapped in some ice and thought he would die. He was set free, just in time, by a farmer and his dog.

Spring came and the lake where he had spent the lonely winter became a busy, exciting, and noisy place. The ducks were forever quacking and the geese were forever honking. There was plenty of splashing and excitement. But not for the ugly duckling. No one quacked the latest piece of gossip to him. Sadly he spread his wings and took to the sky. He had never flown before and he was surprised how strong his wings were. They carried him away from the lake and the marshes and over a leafy garden.

On a still, clear pond in the garden, he could see the beautiful white swans, with their gracefully arched necks, and suddenly the ugly duckling felt that he did not want to live any longer.

''I will go down to the pond and ask those beautiful birds to kill me,'' he said. And down he went to the water. He bent his head humbly and closed his eyes.

233

"Kill me," he said to the swans. "I am too ugly to live."

"Ugly?" said the swans. "Have you looked at your reflection?"

"I do not need to look. I know how ugly I am," said the ugly duckling.

"Look into the water," said the swans. And so the ugly duckling did. What he saw made his heart beat fast and filled him with happiness. During the long winter months he had changed.

"I'm . . . I'm just like you . . ." he whispered.

When the children who lived in the garden came to feed the swans they called to one another,

"A new swan . . . a new swan . . . isn't he beautiful?" And then the ugly duckling knew without a doubt that he really WAS a swan, that he had ALWAYS been a swan and that his days of being lonely were over.

*O*h where, oh where has my little dog gone?
Oh where, oh where can he be?
With his ears cut short and his tail cut long,
Oh where, oh where is he?

There was a crooked man, and he walked a crooked mile,
He found a crooked sixpence against a crooked stile;
He bought a crooked cat,
    which caught a crooked mouse,
    And they all lived together in a little crooked house.